THE ORVIS®

KIDS' GUIDE TO BEGINNING FLY FISHING

EASY TIPS TO
CATCH FISH
TODAY

TYLER BEFUS

FOREWORD BY TOM ROSENBAUER

Sky Pony Press
New York

Sky Pony Press books may be purchased in bulk at special discounts for sales promotion, corporate gifts, fund-raising, or educational purposes. Special editions can also be created to specifications. For details, contact the Special Sales Department, Sky Pony Press, 307 West 36th Street, 11th Floor, New York, NY 10018 or info@skyhorsepublishing.com.

Sky Pony® is a registered trademark of Skyhorse Publishing, Inc.®, a Delaware corporation.

Visit our website at www.skyponypress.com.

10 9 8 7 6 5 4 3 2 1

Manufactured in China, November 2015
This product conforms to CPSIA 2008

Library of Congress Cataloging-in-Publication Data is available on file.

Cover design by Sarah Brody
Cover photo credit Tom Rosenbauer

Print ISBN: 978-1-63450-338-9
Ebook ISBN: 978-1-63450-619-9

CONTENTS

Tyler Befus

FOREWORD

BY TOM ROSENBAUER

You might wonder *What the heck is a guy in his early sixties doing writing a foreword for a kid's guide to fly fishing*? Good question. First, I have a ten-year-old son, so I have some idea what goes through the mind of a kid, although I will admit that I probably only know what Brett is thinking about maybe a quarter of the time. Also, I heard a friend the other day say that fly fishing appeals to grown men and women because it's the only time it's appropriate for us to be twelve years old again. I sure don't disagree with that statement. When I am fishing, all my adult troubles become like wisps of mist from a trout stream waterfall, and the only thing I can concentrate on is looking for bugs in the river, spotting fish lying in wait along an undercut bank, and getting a fish to inhale my fake bug so I can match wits with it, trying to get it into my net and safely back into the water after touching it for a brief moment and maybe snapping a quick photo so I can remember its brilliant colors.

I taught myself to fish with a fly rod when I was about eleven or twelve years old. My father took me fishing as early as a toddler, and he loved to fish, but when I got older he became obsessed with golf. We still fished together, but not as much as we used to, and when I decided fly fishing looked fascinating I knew I would have to learn on my own. I know it's hard for you to imagine, but in those days we had no YouTube, no Internet at all, and we didn't even have DVDs. If you wanted to see fly fishing in action you would either have to find people who were good at it and follow them around, or, once a week, you could watch the TV show "The American Sportsman," where you could see people like Bing Crosby, Curt Gowdy, and Lee Wulff fishing with a fly rod in exotic places around the world. Those names probably don't mean anything to you, but Bing Crosby was one of the most famous singers of the twentieth century, Curt Gowdy was a beloved sports announcer, and Lee Wulff was the most famous fly fisherman in the world. And, no, you couldn't watch this show on demand or record it on TiVo. You got one shot a week, and if you missed it, too bad.

Not a single person in my high school of two thousand kids knew anything about fly fishing. I had one buddy from Boy Scouts who went to another school, and we were able to learn together, borrowing the few books on fly fishing from the library and devouring every issue of *Field & Stream* and *Outdoor Life* magazines, searching for the few articles on fly fishing each year. We practiced casting in our yards and tried to get the hang of fly casting, but we really had no idea what we were doing. We finally joined a local Trout Unlimited chapter when we were sixteen and could drive, and luckily some of the older gentlemen in the chapter (we were the youngest members by at least twenty years) took us under their wings and out on trips to local trout streams. And when I went off to college on a campus of close to twenty thousand students, in the four years I was there I only met one person who was a fly fisher—the teaching assistant in my zoology class. Young people who fished with a fly rod were a rarity, as it was the province of stuffy old guys.

Today, there are fly-fishing classes in elementary schools, fly-fishing clubs in high schools, and large, active fly-fishing student groups on many college campuses. You shouldn't have to look far for some instruction from one of your peers, and I'm sure you'd rather learn from someone your own age than from an old guy like me. Of course, you can also rent or buy DVDs with good fly-fishing instruction, you can stream thousands of hours of great instruction from the web, or you can download helpful podcasts to listen to while driving or cutting the grass (hopefully not during Algebra class, although I know you'll be tempted).

Don't rule out books, either. There are a number of reasons to use books to learn fly fishing as well as visual instructions. First, chances are that books are vetted, because someone paid a lot of money to design and print the book you have in your hands, and you can be sure that publishers make sure the instructions and illustrations in a book are credible and valuable. Otherwise, they would be wasting many thousands of dollars to produce the book. Anybody can upload a video to the web, and although there are some great fly-fishing instructions out there in cyber land, there is also a lot of junk done by bozos who really don't know what they're doing.

I think books are also easier to scan. If you are looking for instructions on a particular area of fly fishing, it's so much easier to quickly page through a book to find exactly what you want. Maybe you don't agree because you'd just use the search function in Google, and maybe I am showing my age by preferring to scan a physical book. But sometimes it's nice to hold a book in your hands, sit back in a comfortable chair, and relax your eyes by getting them away from a screen.

That vetting business I described earlier is especially true for the author of this book, Tyler Befus. The guy has earned his chops and has nothing to prove, because he's already had a rich education in fly fishing. Lucky for Tyler, he has a loving dad who is a superb and patient fly fisher, so Tyler got the head start most of us won't have the opportunity to enjoy. He's fished many places, from the Great Lakes to Japan. In fact, Tyler was invited to Japan to teach fly fishing to elementary school students by Japan's Board of Tourism. You can bet they weren't about to buy an expensive plane ticket for a kid who didn't know anything about instructing fly fishing.

Tyler was also on the USA Youth Fly Fishing Team, probably the highest honor for any kid involved in fly fishing. Competitive fishing is demanding and hard work and it may not appeal to you, but to get on a competitive team like this takes real skill. Lots of kids try out for this team but very few make it, and the kids who do make the team are coached by some of the finest adult fly fishers in the world. Having Tyler share what he's learned in that experience is a great benefit to those of us who read his book.

I really admire the way Tyler presents his information. His writing is clear and concise, and he doesn't overwhelm us with jargon or overly technical descriptions of fly fishing. After all, it's just another way of fishing, and fishing is supposed to be easy and fun, not a chore like schoolwork.

But what I like most about Tyler's book is how he describes the inspiration fly fishing has brought to him in other aspects of his life. He now has friends across the globe, he's learned to be a good photographer, he's traveled extensively, he's learned entomology, and he's even been inspired to paint as a result of his fly-fishing pursuits. You have a real treat ahead of you, and I hope you enjoy as much inspiration from fly fishing as Tyler.

Tyler Befus

PREFACE

The ORVIS Kids' Guide to Beginning Fly Fishing gives an overview of the sport of fly fishing and allows newcomers to learn the basics of my personal favorite sport and activity.

When I was around seven years old, I was spending great amounts of time at fly fishing shows and expositions where I would present and tie flies. One thing that kept coming to mind show after show was the fact that there were very few other kids besides myself in attendance. With my first book, *A Kid's Guide to Fly Fishing*, I hoped to excite other youth—and even their parents or other beginners—about fly fishing and to show that this sport has something that will interest almost all people. Published when I was eight years old, *A Kid's Guide to Fly Fishing* proved to accomplish its task, and over the years, I have seen more and more youth out fly fishing.

Almost a decade later, I have now learned much more from my fly-fishing adventures and from other anglers I have been fortunate enough to meet from all over the world, and I wanted to share some of that information with youth anglers. In order to do so, I figured it was time to rewrite and revamp my first book, which has brought about this wonderful compilation of gear, flies, entomology, casting, fishing techniques, and much more. I hope that as you read this book, you will not only learn how to fly fish, but also grow to love this wonderful sport and adventure. Tight lines!

CHAPTER 1

WHAT IS FLY FISHING?

What, exactly, is fly fishing? Before you can answer this question, you need to know a few basic things. First, you need to know what a fly is. We are not talking about a common house fly, but rather a creation of feathers, fur, yarn, thread, beads, and many other materials tied onto a hook to look like a bug or some other type of food that fish like to eat.

Second, you need to know what fishing actually is. Fishing is an activity that you do when you are trying to catch a fish. You might do this for fun or as a sport. So put fly and fishing together and you get an activity you do with an artificial fly to catch a fish! When you are fly fishing, you will use a fly rod and fly line to cast the fly and to try to make the fly look like a real bug or a fish swimming in the water, so it will fool the fish you are trying to catch.

Now you might ask, what is a fly rod and a fly line? A fly rod is a fishing rod that is generally seven to nine feet long. It is used with a special reel called a fly reel and a line called a fly line. You might think about a spinning or casting reel when you picture a fishing reel. But a fly reel is much simpler than those types of reels. Most of the time the fly reel is just there to hold your fly line, but it does have a braking system called a drag to help you to fight a big fish.

The fly line is unique and different from regular fishing line. Fly line has a braided line as the core that is then covered with a slick plastic coating. This adds weight to the line so that it can be cast effortlessly with the fly rod. You will learn more about fly rods, fly reels, and fly lines later in the book.

Before you begin, you also need to learn the difference between fly casting and bait casting (also called spin casting). Other types of fishing use weight on the line, usually in the form of a lure or bait, to make the line travel out into the water when you cast. Fly casting, however, uses the weight of the fly line to make the cast and to deliver your fly to the water. This is called "presenting the fly," or "presentation of the fly." The weighted line makes the rod bend while moving the rod back and forth in the air. This action is called "loading the rod." Letting a little bit of the line out with each movement of the rod creates the momentum needed to develop the cast.

Generally, there is a tapered leader, which is a single strand of nylon fiber (called monofilament) that tapers from a thick end to a thin end. This is attached to the end of the fly line. The leader presents the fly on the water like a real bug as it allows for the line to roll out gracefully.

I asked some of my fishing friends for their descriptions of fly fishing to share with you, so you can see the many things that fly fishing has to offer. Here is what some of my friends said about fly fishing:

- "The art of fooling fish while having fun." —Jon Spiegel, Boulder, Colorado
- "Fly fishing is an incredible sport that requires a high level of knowledge and skill to lure and catch fish in beautiful settings and to overcome vastly different scenarios to accomplish goals. But above all, this talent has been given to me as an avenue through which the Gospel can be spread and the truth about Jesus Christ be proclaimed to all people!" —Mason Sims, Chickamauga, Georgia
- "Fly fishing is the thrill of overcoming obstacles both big and small, to experience big, wild, and hard earned successes and failures, but always to win." —Daniel Holm, Denmark
- "Fly fishing is freedom; freedom to explore the world and experience nature." —David S. Heller, Denver, Colorado
- "Fly fishing is trying to catch a fish with an imitation of an insect, an imitation that we have made ourselves." —Martin Westbeek, Oisterwijk, Holland

- "Fly fishing is just a good reason to get out and enjoy nature. It brings you in contact with the river, fish, insect life, weather, and the environment in general—causing you to focus on all of these instead of yourself."
—Tom Whiting, Delta, Colorado

I believe that fly fishing is an adventure that includes spending time outdoors learning about nature with your family and friends—and it is sometimes about catching fish. Fly fishing is a sport and an art form that uses a rod and line to cast a fly to a fish and to trick the fish into eating that fly. There is not a right or wrong answer to the question, "What is fly fishing?" Different people fly fish for different reasons, and there are different parts of fly fishing that people find more interesting than others.

One of my early fishing experiences from the backpack carrier.

Fly fishing has been a way of life for me and my family for as long as I can remember. Some of the first trips I went on were with my mom and dad just a few months after I was born—once I was finally big enough to ride in a baby backpack carrier. I would try to cast and hook a fish from the backpack. Well, actually, my dad would hook the fish then let me fight them and try to land them.

There is much more to fly fishing than the equipment and the fish. When you are a fly fisher you learn about bugs, the outdoors, fish, the currents in a river, fly tying, fly casting, photography, art, wildlife, and traveling to different places. If you like adventures, then you will love fly fishing.

Throughout this book, I hope to teach you about fly fishing as well as share some of my own personal experiences. When I was six years old, I experienced my first big trip outside of Colorado. Being the middle of winter, I was a little bit fishing deprived and was daydreaming of warmer weather and days on the river often.

One day, my dad asked me if I wanted to take a trip to Alaska that summer to fish for northern pike and sheefish, which is the largest member of the whitefish family. (Some fish have very funny names as you will see later in the book.) Without hesitating, I said yes and was ready to start preparing for the trip. The first order of business was to get all of my flies tied. Hours later, my dad and I had dozens of flies tied up and in boxes ready to be packed.

Next, we made sure we had all of our gear and clothing ready for a whole week of fishing.

It was a lot of work but after months of waiting and preparing, June finally arrived, and it was time to get on an airplane to head north to Alaska. We had to fly on four different airplanes to get to the fishing spot. The flight that stands out most in my memory was the final leg of the journey, when we flew in a float plane (these take off and land on the water, which, to me, makes them even more awesome).

We stayed at my Uncle Greg's lodge, which is a sixty-seven-foot-long house boat located on the Innoko River. My good friend Pat Oglesby made the trip with us and my Aunt Laure and cousins Jacob and Travis even came out for the week. Never having been guided for a fishing trip before, I didn't know quite what to think of having someone to boat me around to the different fishing spots and to help out whenever it was needed, but by the end of the trip, I had become pretty good friends with both Ross and Jason. After getting settled in at the lodge, unpacking, rigging up, and donning our waders, it was time to go fishing.

We fished from a small boat that Ross, our guide, used in order to take us to different fishing spots. He even let me drive the boat with his help! I made sure to wear my life jacket to make certain I would be safe in case I fell overboard. That first night, Ross took us to a spot where I caught my first northern pike. It was twenty

Me and the float plane we used.

My uncle, aunt, a few of my new friends, and the houseboat that we stayed on in the Innoko River.

inches long and had razor sharp teeth. My dad snapped a couple pictures and then we released it back into the water.

During the week, I got to fly in the floatplane with my dad and our pilot, Ron, to other places to fish. Ron said I was his youngest passenger ever. Flying to new areas throughout the day gave me the opportunity to scan the ground and water for wildlife, which included everything from eagles with a freshly caught fish to bears and even moose. The meals we had were delicious as all of the fish were fresh caught. On one unfortunate occasion, I was offered Eskimo ice cream that is made from mashed up whitefish, blueberries, and Crisco. Of course I thought it would be fun to try a new food, but it only took one spoonful to get me to stop eating. Suffice it to say, it is a memory that I cringe at every time I think back on it.

Each morning before going fishing I would take time to write in my trip journal, which my mom put together for me, about my experiences from the day before so I would always remember my trip there.

Some days we would fish very late into the evening—even as late as one o'clock in the morning! It barely gets dark in Alaska during June, so it was easy to lose track of what time of day it was.

The first northern pike I caught on the trip.

The weather changed constantly, too. It was sunny, then cloudy, then rainy. The wind would blow and then the sun would come back out. Fortunately, we were prepared and the fishing continued. We landed fish every day with my biggest pike of the trip measuring thirty-three inches, which I caught on a fly I tied myself. The last day we fished, it was raining and pretty cold. Then a rainbow appeared in the sky, and I found my pot of gold underneath it. After many missed casts and failed hook ups, I caught a seven-pound sheefish, which beat the previous record and still stands as the International Gamefish Association (IGFA) junior angler world record.

That fishing trip to Alaska was amazing and one I will never forget. It was a true adventure—just like every time I go fishing. A fly-fishing adventure can be just a couple of hours at a local pond catching bluegill, or a full day on the river fishing for trout, or even a weeklong trip to Alaska or somewhere else in the world. To start your own adventures in fly fishing, turn the page to learn more about this amazing activity.

My dad and me with the seven-pound sheefish I was blessed with catching.

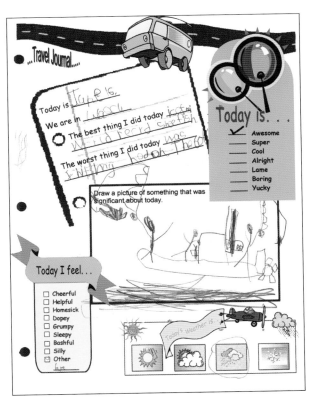

A page from the fishing journal my mom put together for me to use on the trip.

CHAPTER 2

THE FISH

Fish are a very important part to fly fishing, because without them, we would not be able to fish at all! What I enjoy most about this part of the sport is that every fish is different—different sizes, colors, and shapes—and they are found in so many different locations. No matter where you are in the world, there are almost always fish to be caught: marlin in Costa Rica,

My sister Vivian with a white bass.

yamame in Japan, trout in Montana, bass on a local pond, or even sight fishing for carp in the heart of a big city. If you are willing to search for them and put in the effort to get there, you will almost always be able to find some sort of fishing spot full of fish.

Learning about Fish

Fish need certain things in order to survive. They need clean water, food, and places to hide for protection. Most fish like to live by some kind of structure that can be natural, like rocks, weed beds, a floating log, or an undercut bank. A tree overhanging the water or even clouds in the sky, which reduce the amount of light reflecting on the water, can be considered cover that fish like. Manmade structures providing protection for fish can include such things as a dock, a shipwreck in the ocean, or big pieces of concrete used to reinforce a bank in a river.

It is also fun to learn the names of different parts of a fish. Check out the diagram at the top of the next page and test to see how many parts of a fish you already know!

Most beginning fly fishers learn to fish for panfish, bass, or trout because these types of fish are some of the most readily available to catch. Let's learn a little more about each of these fish before you set out on your fly-fishing adventures!

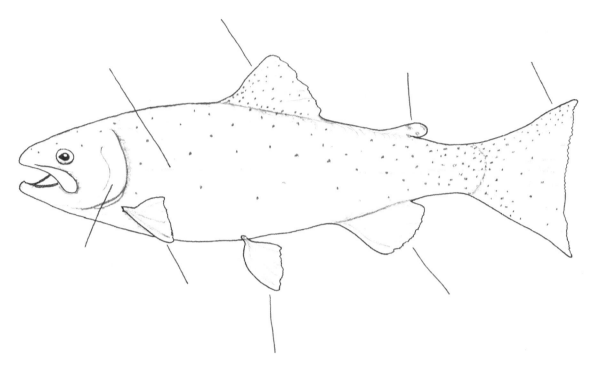

Answer Key (starting from the top and moving clockwise): lateral line, dorsal fin, adipose fin, caudal fin, anal fin, pelvic fin, pectoral fin, gill cover.

Panfish

Panfish is a common term used to describe a group of fish that live in freshwater. Types of panfish include bluegill, crappie, yellow perch, and various sunfishes. Panfish are found all over the United States—from city park lakes to thousands of farm ponds. They are a great fish to learn to fly fish on because they are easy to find, are extremely willing to eat a fly, and do not require a perfect cast to fool them. Even though they usually do not grow very large, panfish can really pull hard and give a good fight, too.

Most panfish spend much of their time in shallow water and many times you can see the fish you are casting your fly to, which is called "sight fishing." Being one of the smaller game fish in the water means that panfish like to spend a lot of time around structures. Often times even a small stump in the water will provide enough cover for a couple of fish.

Panfish are also a good type of fish on which to practice your fish handling skills and hook removal skills. The reason for this is that they are a pretty tough fish. Nonetheless, it is always important to treat every fish with lots of respect. If you are going to release the fish you catch, this is especially true. If you are not careful with the way you handle fish, you may end up hurting them. And as a side note, if you kill the fish you hook, you will never have the fun of catching that same fish again, and for this reason, I am a strong supporter of catch and release fishing practices.

A bluegill was actually the first fish I caught on a fly rod. When I was just two years old, I was fishing

After a debate tournament, my sister Olivia and I did some bluegill fishing in a nearby pond.

at a small lake named Chipeta Lake in Montrose, Colorado, with my mom and dad. With their help, I caught my first bluegill! My parents say that I was very excited at the time and that catching the bluegill is the probably the reason I kept fly fishing and love this activity so much.

To this day, one of my favorite fish to fish for is the green sunfish. There was a lake that was about twenty minutes' drive from my home in Colorado. The lake had thousands of green sunfish living in it. During the summer, my family and I would fish there a couple times a week after my dad got home from work. My five-year-old sister, Ava, and I would have contests to see who could catch more green sunfish. Some evenings we would catch as many as forty or fifty of them in just a few hours—that was when the fishing was red hot.

Because of how often we were fishing at the lake, I developed my own fly pattern to use for these cool fish and named it the "Secret Weapon."

A few of our little contests were won on this fly alone and I soon found out that it worked for all sorts of fish, including yellow perch, bass, bluegill,

The original "Secret Weapon" design.

Tips for Handling Fish When You Are Going to Release Them
- Always try to land the fish quickly so they do not get too tired out.
- Try to use a net whenever possible to help land the fish.
- Wet your hands before touching the fish so you do not rub off their protective slimy coating.
- Never squeeze a fish.
- Try to keep the fish in the water when you remove the hook (using barbless hooks or a hook with the barb pinched down will make it easier to remove the hook).
- Do not keep the fish out of the water for too long if you want to take a picture of them (they cannot breathe out of the water).
- Make sure the fish is strong enough to swim away before releasing it.

carp, trout, and, of course, green sunfish. I'll talk more about tying your own flies later in the book.

Bass

Bass are larger members of the panfish family and also live in freshwater streams and lakes. Some of the most popular and

Smallmouth bass.

readily accessible bass include smallmouth, largemouth, and spotted bass. Just like panfish, bass are also very aggressive toward artificial flies, making them a good fish on which to practice fly fishing. Bass have the ability grow quite large in the right conditions, giving the fly fisher a chance at catching a really big fish.

A bass's diet will mainly include smaller fish, crayfish, and bugs that live in the water. Many bass flies are designed to look like baitfish, worms, and leeches. Bass flies are arguably some of the most creative. One of the most traditional and well-known fly style used for bass fishing are poppers. These are flies made out of cork, foam, or deer hair that float and make a "popping" or "gurgling" sound when the line is pulled and the fly moves on the surface of the water.

Bass like to spend time around structures so that they can ambush other fish, frogs, crayfish, and bugs—just like the panfish. Fishing with poppers at night can be a productive way to catch bass as they do not feel threatened by moving away from their structure.

This is just one more adventure you can have when fly fishing. Besides the bass, there are lots of other animals that come out at night, which can make your time fishing even more exciting.

Trout

There are four basic kinds of trout: rainbow trout, brown trout, cutthroat trout, and brook trout. Trout live in cool or cold freshwater lakes, ponds, streams, and rivers. A trout's main source of food is insects that live in the water, such as mayflies, caddis flies, stoneflies, and midges (you will learn more about these later in the book). When the opportunity presents itself, trout will also eat small fish or minnows, leeches, crayfish, freshwater shrimp, and aquatic worms. Many insects that live on land are also favorite foods of the trout. These include ants, beetles, grasshoppers, and crickets.

In lakes, trout live by different types of structures and will cruise around looking for food. In streams and rivers, trout mostly stay in one area and wait for the current in the water to bring food to them.

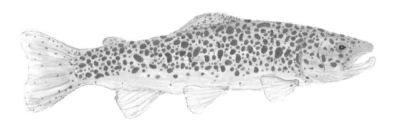

Brown trout.

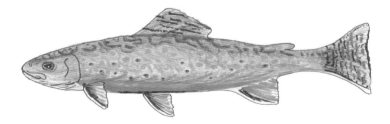

Brook trout.

Rainbow trout.

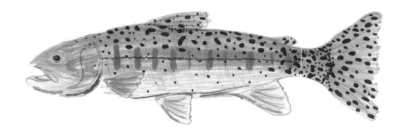

Cutthroat trout.

Rainbow trout.

Cutthroat trout.

Brook trout.

Brown trout.

My very first muskellunge.

© Tyler Befus

Sturgeon.

Striped bass.

A giant carp caught by my dad.

Largemouth bass.

My sister Ava with a king salmon.

Northern pike.

Kokanee salmon.

Tarpon.

Sailfish.

Black crappie.

A yamame caught all the
way in Japan.

CHAPTER 3

FINDING FISH

There is a little more you need to understand about fish before you start fly fishing. Fish have certain places where they like to live and feed—mainly in lakes and in streams. If you know what and where these places are, it will be a lot easier for you to catch them.

Understanding the Places Fish Live in Rivers and Streams

Remember from the last chapter that fish like to live around structures. Rivers and streams usually have many different types of structures where fish will live. Different types of water currents create different types of structure where fish feel safe from predators or can find food. Bugs that are living in the rocks and gravel get washed away by the current, and the fish eat them as they float downstream or toward their hiding place.

If you understand what these water currents do, you can then use these currents to know where the fish are. This is called "reading the water." It is sort of like reading a map. There are many different types of currents in a river or stream. Below are the names of these different types of currents as well as descriptions of the water types where you can find fish in a river or stream.

Riffle

A riffle is a shallow area that has fast-moving water flowing over the rocks on the bottom. This makes the water look choppy on the surface. Riffles are also bug factories because the faster current keeps more oxygen in the water. Trout use riffles to feed in during

Fishing a typical riffle.

the summer, when there is enough water to give the fish some protection. During the winter, when the water levels are lower, you will usually not find trout in riffles.

Run

A run is a deeper water section with some larger rocks. Runs can be fast or slow, and are a good place for fish to find protection because the water is deeper and the surface is choppy. This makes it harder for predators to see the fish. Trout use runs to feed in all year long as well as a place for safety.

One of my favorite runs on the Colorado River in Colorado.

A run can be teaming with fish . . . it is catching them that seems to be the trick.

Pool

A pool is an area of deeper water that has a slow-moving current. Sometimes there are large rocks in a pool that provide structure for fish to live near. When the water levels are lower in the riffles or a shallow run, trout will use pools as their home. Trout will also feed in pools all year long, just like in a run.

A deep pool.

Pocket Water

Pocket water is an area that has rocks sticking out of the water in the current, which creates areas of slower water behind them called

Pocket water on a small stream in Japan.

pockets. These pockets are good places for trout to sit and wait for food to come drifting by so they can eat it. Pocket water can be in a riffle, run, or pool.

Current Seams

Current seams are places where fast and slow water come together. Current seams are found in both shallow and deep water in a river or a stream. In fast water there will usually be a lot of food for fish. Trout, for example, can sit in the slower water and

Current seams can be very easy to see, like in this example, but other times it takes a little more patience and effort to find them.

Here I am nymphing a current seam right along the bank.

eat the bugs as they float by in the current. In pocket water, there are current seams created by the rocks sticking above the surface. Current seams are my favorite type of water to fly fish for trout, because I catch a lot of fish in them.

Eddy

An eddy is a current that spins in a circle. It is created by different speeds of water coming together, usually in a spot where the river turns or has a bend. Eddies create spots that collect a lot of the bugs floating down the river and are also a great place for minnows or smaller fish to stay in order to avoid the fast current. Fish are

Eddies can often be spotted by the collection of bubbles on the water's surface.

very likely to hang out close to or in eddies due to an almost buffet-style meal that can be present there.

Understanding the Places Fish Live in Lakes and Ponds

Since lakes generally do not have moving water, the fish who live in them have to move around more in search of their food. It is important for you to know where the bugs and small minnows, or baitfish, generally live in a lake so you can find where the trout or bass will be when fishing a lake or pond. There are some things you can look at to understand, or "read," a lake or pond just like you can with a river or stream so you are sure to find fish to catch.

Inlets

An inlet is the place where a stream or river flows into a lake. Fish like inlets because many food items are washed into the lake by the river or stream's current as it flows into the lake or pond. Lakes usually have at least one inlet but it is possible to have multiple inlets.

An inlet into Lake Superior. Even in lakes as large as the Great Lakes, an inlet is a main attraction to all sorts of fish.

Weed beds

Weed beds are found in a lake or pond's shallow and deep water. Weed beds consist of plants that grow in the water. They make a home for bugs and minnows that live in a lake and also provide structure for trout, bluegill, bass,

A lake with lots of weed beds for fish to hide and feed in.

and other gamefish that you are trying to catch. (According to *McClane's New Standard Fishing Encyclopedia*, "a Gamefish is defined as any type of fish that can be taken by sporting methods.")

Ledges or Drop-Offs

Ledges and drop-offs are places where the shoreline or rocks or other structure create a shelf—somewhat like the ones in a closet. There can be a flat spot and then the bottom of the lake just drops off into deeper water. These are places that predator fish (meaning any fish that will chase down or ambush other fish) such as pike, bass, trout, or musky will launch a surprise attack on smaller fish or minnows that swim off the shelf and into deeper water. Sometimes these drop-offs create a water temperature change in a lake. All fish living in lakes have a water temperature that they are most comfortable living in. As the seasons change, fish will move around a pond or lake to different depths of water in order to stay comfortable.

Fishing along steep drop-offs into the water, like near these dock pilings, can be some great fishing.

Points

A point is a piece of land that goes out into the water from a lake or pond's bank or shoreline. Points can also extend out into or under the water. This creates a high spot that the fish will use as a structure. Sometimes there can be drop-offs or ledges created by a point. Smaller fish will use the point as a safe place to hide, away from the deep water. This will cause the big fish to come

Even a smaller point like this one provides plenty of cover for fish to be lurking around waiting for their next meal.

toward the point looking for a meal. If a point is rocky, has some weed beds around it, or contains some other sort of structure, then it will attract more fish food, which will lead to more fish swimming around the point.

Shorelines

If you are looking at the land around a lake, you can learn a lot about what is under the water. If there is a steep, rocky bank that goes right to the edge of the water, it is usually going to make a steep drop-off under the water. If the shoreline is flat or has a gradual slope to the shoreline, it is most likely going to be shallow some distance

A shoreline can tell you a lot about what is going to be under the surface of the water. Steep shorelines usually lead to deeper water and flatter or more gradually sloped shores will mean shallower water.

from the bank out into the lake. A steep shoreline can be a spot where fish like trout, bass, and panfish like to be, because there is deep water close by for them to hide in. Sometimes these shorelines will have food items stacked up on them as well. If the wind is blowing against that steep shoreline, it will push bugs like ants, beetles, and grasshoppers against it and the fish will come there to eat them.

Manmade lakes and ponds have dams that hold back the water. Sometimes these dams have rocks or concrete along them that creates a structure for fish to hang around.

All fish will use structure for protection. Can you see the trout in this photo using the weeds, rocks, and nearby branches as cover?

These are also steep shoreline areas that are likely to produce fish that you can try to catch.

Where I grew up in Colorado, there was a small ranch that I fished on that had a handful of lakes, and a few of them had some really large fish! I often had my best success fishing from the dams. The trout would spend their time cruising close to the dam looking for food. If I cast flies that looked like small fish and leeches, the trout couldn't resist and would almost always end up devouring my fly at some point. One day I caught seven trout that weighed over five pounds—the heaviest being eight pounds—from one of the small lakes using this technique. It makes sense, because if a really big trout sees a small fish swimming in the deep water that is out from the dam, the small fish will make an easy meal for the trout.

CHAPTER 4

THE GEAR

Gathering my fly-fishing gear throughout the years has been almost as much fun as the fishing part itself. My first fly rod was an ice fishing rod that my dad put a fly reel and fly line on for me to start casting with. It was an excellent learning rod due to its light weight and short length, which made it easier for my young arms to control.

A trip to the local discount store with my dad produced a pair of knee-high rubber boots. Yes, my first pair of waders, and I had only been walking for a year and a half! I should mention that all anglers, young and old, need to be very careful when wading in the water. Our family rule is that we never get into the water unless a parent is with us and stays within arm's reach until we are of a certain age and wading capability.

As I learned early on, it isn't necessary to spend a lot of money to start fly fishing. There are only a few basic pieces of must-have gear to get in order to start fly fishing. In addition to the necessities, there are other pieces of gear that will make your fishing experience more enjoyable. Some of the pieces of gear have very funny names as you will see in a little while.

The following two lists of equipment show necessary items to get started with and items that will make your fly-fishing adventure more enjoyable. I have included a description of each of these different items so you will know what I am talking about later in the book. Some of these items are things your mom and dad will be responsible for getting together for you before getting out on the water.

Must-Have List

These items are essential to starting fly fishing.

- **Fly rod.** A fly rod, usually seven to ten feet in length, is longer than the average spinning or casting rod. Fly rods come in all different line sizes, which allows you to fish for different fish species that may require a larger or smaller weight rod in order to give them a fighting chance. For

My first fly rod was an ice fishing rod with a fly reel, but eventually I upgraded to a standard-sized rod.

example, a four-weight or five-weight rod is a good line size to start with, because it is able to catch a variety of fish, from trout to sunfish to bass—and even some larger fish such as carp.

- **Fly reel.** A fly reel holds the line and backing. (Backing is a braided line that goes on your reel before the fly line. It is a filler for the reel and gives you extra line if a big fish takes out all the fly line.) Fly reels come in different sizes, just like fly rods. Generally, fly reels have an adjustable drag to help you land larger fish.

Fly reels are not overly complicated and are mainly used for holding the line and, at times, for fighting big fish.

If you are pursuing really big fish, a fly reel with a good drag is important. The drag of the reel makes it harder for the fish to pull off line from the reel, which tires the fish out, making it easier to land them. This not only makes the fight less prolonged, but it is also a lot better for the fish.

- **Fly line.** The fly line has a braided inside with a slick plastic coating. Some fly lines are made to float, and some are made to sink. The fly line is different from regular fishing line because it is bigger around and is also weighted. Remember,

Picking the right fly line is crucial when finding your gear, because it can often make or break a day on the water.

it is the weight of the line that bends, or loads, the rod when you are casting. Fly lines come in many different colors ranging from dark green and gray to black or colors like chartreuse and blue. I like brightly colored lines because they are easier to see and help me know where my fly is in the water. Since there are so many types of lines, it is important to find the right one for you. The key component is getting a line that matches the weight of the rod. (If you have a four-weight rod, you should use a four-weight fly line to help the rod cast properly.) If the fly line is too heavy or too light for your rod, it makes it hard to cast.

- **Tapered leader.** A tapered leader is tied to the end of your fly line and is made out of monofilament (basically, this is fishing line but it is tapered from thick to thin). The reason that the leader is tapered is to help your cast by turning over the line and allowing it to lay straight on the water. If you tied on regular fishing line to your rod, the cast would pile up in front of you and the fly would never end up reaching the fish. The last part of the leader is called the tippet. The tippet is not tapered and is where you tie on your fly. When the tippet is broken or used up from tying knots while changing flies, it can be replaced with a new tippet. You will be learning the basic knots later in this chapter. The leader is clear so that the fish do not see it when you are trying to fool them with your fly.

There are all different sizes of leader and tippet so it is easy to find the right kind for the fish you are targeting.

- **Flies.** There are three main types of flies that you can fish. The first are dry flies, which float on top of the water. Next, there are nymphs, which sink and imitate insects that live in the water. Last, but certainly not least, are streamers, which are meant to look like larger fish food that lives in the water—such as minnows or crayfish. Within these three categories, there are literally thousands of different fly patterns. Depending on the water type, species of fish you are fishing for, the season, and what

Flies come in all different sizes, shapes, and colors. Here are streamers, nymphs, dry flies, and wet flies.

part of the world you are in, you can then determine the type of flies you should fish.

- **Hat or baseball cap.** A hat is important to protect you from the sun and to protect you from hooking yourself when you cast.

- **Polarized sunglasses.** Polarized sunglasses help you see your fly and help you see fish, because they remove the glare that the sun makes on the water's surface. If you do not have polarized sunglasses, it's okay, but it is still important to wear what you have in order to protect your eyes from being hooked when casting. Another family rule of mine is that we can never cast unless we have on our sunglasses.

- **Sunscreen and insect repellent.** It is very easy to get sunburned when you are by the water fishing all day. For this reason, it is important to use sunscreen. Insect repellent is also good to have with you so if the mosquitoes start to bite, you can put it on and still enjoy your fly-fishing trip. Since some insect repellents have bad chemicals in them, be sure to only apply this to your hat and clothing to keep the bugs away. Wearing a long-sleeved shirt helps protect you from the sun and from the bugs and also minimizes the amount of chemicals that can get on your skin from the sunscreen or insect repellent.

- **Fishing license.** In some places a fishing license is required for kids. It is important to have your parents check the rules and laws in your area before you go fishing.

Nice-to-Have List

These items will make your fly-fishing experience more enjoyable.

While not all of this gear is necessary, it can make your fly-fishing experience more enjoyable.

- **Split shot.** Small lead or tin weights used on the leader to help sink flies.
- **Fly floatant.** Most fly floatant is like a paste that you put on flies to help them float on the surface and to help keep them dry.
- **Strike indicator.** This is really just a fancy word for a bobber. Strike indicators come in all different sizes, colors, and shapes. They go on your leader to help you know when a fish eats your wet fly or nymph. You will learn more about these later in the book.
- **Fly box.** A fly box is a box used to store your flies when you are fishing. Some fly boxes have foam to stick flies into while

others have compartments to store flies. Basically, any small plastic box will work as a fly box.

A hat, long-sleeve shirt, sunglasses, and a Buff, bandana, or other similar product can really help to keep the sun off your upper body.

- **Waders.** Waders keep you dry and warm when you are standing in the water fly fishing. While it can be a lot of fun to wade in just shorts and an old pair of sneakers during the summer months, habits like that can get very cold very quickly once fall and winter set in.

- **Long-sleeved shirt.** Sleeves protect your arms from sunburn and from mosquito bites.

- **Rain jacket.** This is good to have just in case it rains when you are on one of your big adventures.

- **Line clippers.** These are small clippers like a fingernail clipper that are used to trim line when tying knots. These clippers are much safer than scissors or a pocket knife.

- **Hemostats/Forceps.** This is another special item for fly fishers to help remove flies from the fish's mouth. They can also be used to pinch split shot onto the leader and to bend down barbs on your hooks to make them easier to remove from the fish.

- **Camera.** It is fun to take a picture of the big fish that did not get away to show your friends and family.

All covered up.

- **Landing net.** This makes it easier to land your fish.

CHAPTER 5

THE METHODS

It's time to talk about the different methods or techniques used to catch fish when fly fishing. There are lots and lots of different methods to use in different situations you will face on the water. Before you learn the specific fishing techniques, though, it is important to first know how to properly present the fly.

Casting Methods

Fly casting is one of the most important aspects of the sport of fly fishing. If you do not practice casting, you will have a hard time catching fish. That's because you must cast your fly onto the water in order to be successful. When you cast your fly, it is important to have good control of your rod, line, leader, and fly. This

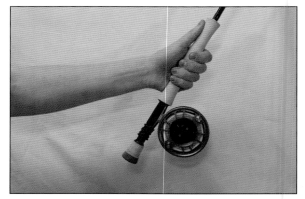

This is how I like to hold the rod grip.

will help with casting accuracy so you will be able to cast the fly where you want it to go on the water.

The first type of cast you need to learn is the most basic: the overhead cast. Once you learn how to make an overhead cast, you can learn other more difficult casts, like curve casts, reach casts, and s-casts. It is always best to practice your casting on the water, but you can also learn how to cast on the grass at the park or in your yard. I recommend taking a casting class from an instructor in your area or through a local fly shop. This will ensure that you are not developing bad habits that can come back to bite you on the water when you are fly fishing. Also, practice your casting. You must practice to become a good fly caster just like playing a sport requires practice.

Overhead Cast

To start practicing an overhead cast, you need to first become friends with your rod. You should hold the grip of the rod in a way that is comfortable for you. You do not need to squeeze the grip so tightly that your hand feels like it will fall off. Remember: fly fishing is supposed to be fun. I like to think of the rod grip as a hammer when I hold it in my hand with my thumb on top of the grip. This is a comfortable way for me to hold it. You may find something that works better for you. Start this overhead casting lesson with a short amount of line on the ground in front of you (maybe ten to fifteen feet of line only).

It is important to have a leader tied onto the end of your fly line and a small piece of yarn tied to the end of your leader. This will help your cast unroll more easily than if you practice with only the fly line. When you practice casting, especially when you are first starting out, you will not want to tie a fly on just to make sure you won't hook yourself.

There is an easy way to understand the places where you should stop the rod when you are casting in order to make good casts. If you imagine the numbers of a clock around you with twelve o'clock being straight above your head, this will help you understand the instructions to learn how to overhead cast.

- **Step 1:** Begin with the rod tip down low so it is close to the water (or the grass). Then, lift the rod tip up, starting slowly; then start accelerating. The fly line in front of you will follow the rod, moving up into the air. The weight of the fly line will start to load the rod (remember, this is when the rod bends).
- **Step 2:** Keep lifting the rod until the rod tip is slightly behind you (imagine between ten and eleven o'clock), and then stop moving the rod. When you stop the rod, this will form a loop in the fly line as it unrolls off the tip of the rod. This is called

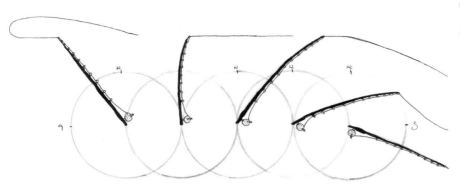

This is the first part of the overhead cast.

the back cast. It is important that this stop is firm and does not allow the rod to continue traveling backwards.

• **Step 3:** Wait just a moment to allow the loop to straighten out behind you (remember to keep the rod tip at about ten o'clock while you are waiting). Make sure you do not wait too long or the line will start to fall onto the ground behind you. Once the loop completely rolls out, then you can start to move your rod arm forward and stop the rod tip just slightly in front of yourself. The weight of the line will bend, or load, the rod as you come forward, which will help the line lay out straight. When you stop the rod in front of you (stop the tip of the rod at about two o'clock), it will form a loop. This is called the forward cast.

• **Step 4:** As the loop unrolls and straightens out, you can then start dropping your rod tip slowly as the line falls back to the water. This will complete the cast and deliver the fly onto the water (or grass).

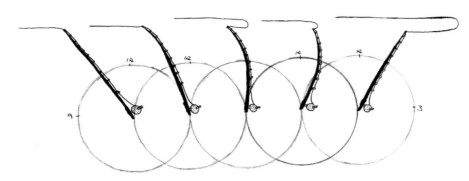

The second and final part of making an overhead cast.

Now, let's say you were using an overhead cast to cast your fly behind a rock in a stream and you want to make some casts to a different location. You can use false casts to change the direction of your cast. False casting is when you keep the fly line in the air without letting it touch the ground or the water. To achieve a false cast, you keep moving the rod between ten o'clock and two o'clock while you move the direction of your cast toward the direction of your next target. It will take a couple false casts to do this, but ultimately, it makes the whole process of changing the direction of your cast much easier and faster.

Fly casting is almost as fun as fishing. To become proficient at fly casting, it is very important to practice your casting as much as possible. The better you become at casting, the more fish you will catch when you are out fishing and the more fun you will have when you can place your fly right where you want it to be. Even better, you will not have to unhook you flies from trees and branches nearly as often!

Here is a fun casting game to play: Pick a place to stand in your yard or on the grass at the park. Put paper plates or pots or pans from the kitchen at varying distances and locations in front of the place you will be standing. Place some to your right, some to your left, some close to you, and some farther away. You can then try to cast your piece of yarn onto the plates or into the pots and pans. This is a fun way to test your skills. You can take turns with friends and even keep score to see who can place their fly in the right spot more often.

Sometimes, it is not possible to make a back cast because there will be bushes, trees, rocks, and other objects behind you that you will hit or tangle your line in. If it is low bushes or a low bank on a river, you must stop your back cast higher in the air to keep your line above those obstacles. When you cannot use a back cast, there is another approach you can use: the roll cast. The roll cast must be practiced on water because the water actually helps load the rod. Here is how you can make a roll cast.

Roll Cast

- **Step 1:** Hold your rod grip the same way you did for the overhead cast and start with about fifteen to twenty feet

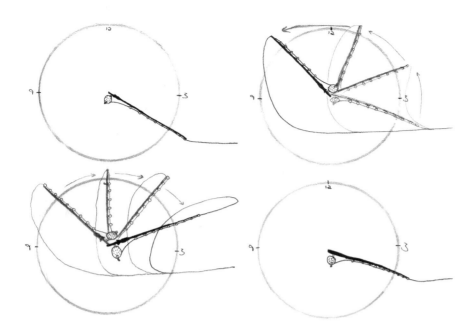

The roll cast is a great technique for casting in tighter spaces.

of fly line on the water and your rod tip down close to the water.

- **Step 2:** Slowly lift your rod tip up and back without making the fly line leave the water. Lift the rod tip to about ten o'clock behind you and allow the loop of fly line to come up beside your casting arm.
- **Step 3:** Once the loop of line stops traveling backwards, you then move your arm forward and down with some power and speed (it is kind of like hitting a nail with a hammer). The water keeps resistance on the fly line and this is what bends, or loads, the rod to make the power of the cast. Make sure to stop the rod tip before it hits the water (stop the rod tip at about three or four o'clock) when making the forward cast with this method. If it does hit the water, you know you went

too far. When the rod tip stops, it will cause the line to unroll on the water in front of you.

And that is the roll cast. The roll cast is a very useful cast when fishing in small streams that do not have much room for an overhead cast. It is also a simple, fast, and effective technique.

Tying Knots

Before you start to learn more about fly-fishing techniques, you need to understand how to tie a couple of important knots so that you can tie tippet onto your leader and to also tie flies onto your tippet. The first knot you need to learn is called the **Double Surgeon Knot**. You can use this knot to tie the tippet onto your leader.

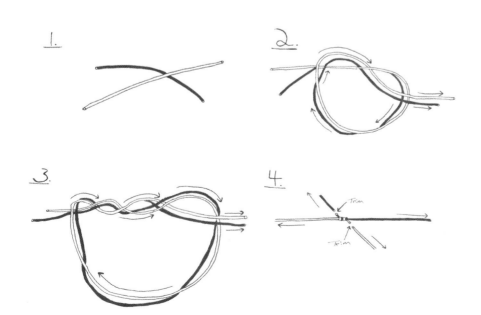

The Double Surgeon Knot is a great knot for tying new tippet onto your leader or even for tying two different pieces of tippet together.

- **Step 1:** Place the leader and the tippet side by side so they are overlapping about six inches.
- **Step 2:** Now, make a loop with the two pieces and pass the end of the leader and the entire tippet through the loop.
- **Step 3:** Pass the same two pieces through the loop one more time. Then wet the knot with some spit or water. This will act as lubricant and will keep the line from weakening or breaking from the friction created when the knot is tightened.
- **Step 4:** Pull all four ends at the same time to start to tighten the knot. Finish tightening the knot by pulling the two short ends. Then trim the two tag ends (the short ends) close to the knot.

Now let's learn how to tie your fly onto the tippet with a **Clinch Knot**. This is a fast, easy knot that is quite strong.

- **Step 1:** Put the tippet through the eye of the hook. Place about six inches through the hook eye, and then lay it side by side with the long piece of tippet.
- **Step 2:** Wrap the short end around the long piece of tippet four to six times, and then place the short end through the small opening in front of the hook eye.

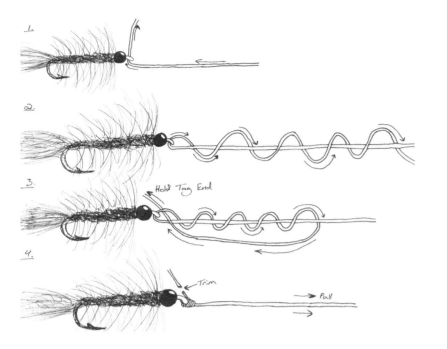

You can use the Clinch Knot to tie your flies onto the tippet.

- **Step 3:** Wet the line with some spit or water, and then slowly pull on the long piece of tippet. Do not start pulling on the short end of the tippet or the knot will not tighten and therefore cannot be strong.
- **Step 4:** Once the knot is tightened, trim the short end close to the knot. Now you are ready to start fishing!

Fly-Fishing Techniques and Methods

There are many different methods and techniques for fly fishing that can be used to catch fish. You need to understand that fishing in rivers or moving water uses different techniques than if you are fishing in lakes or still water. In rivers, the bugs and insects float or drift in the water's current. In lakes, the bugs and insects swim in the water to move around. Small minnows, leeches, and crayfish will swim in both rivers and lakes.

When you start fishing in rivers, you usually want your flies to drift like the natural insects so that the fish will be fooled by them. This is called a "drag-free drift." You can fish flies on the surface, known as "dry-fly fishing," or you can fish flies below the surface, which is called "wet-fly fishing" or "nymph fishing." When you are stripping a fly (pulling line in with your non-casting hand once the fly has been cast into the water) to make it look like a small minnow or baitfish, this is called "streamer fishing." Now it's time to learn how to use some of these different methods.

Dry-fly Fishing

Dry flies usually work best when there is a hatch. A hatch is when the bugs that live in the water or in the rocks and vegetation at the bottom of a lake or stream swim to the top of the water and become flying insects. When this happens, fish generally rise to the surface and feed on the adult bugs, which is called "rising."

When dry-fly fishing on rivers, you will cast your fly above (upstream) from where the fish are rising and let the current carry the fly down to the fish. If you have matched the bug with the right pattern and size fly, you might fool the fish. It is important to let your fly drift to the fish like a natural bug. If it is dragging or skating on the surface, the fish may not eat your fly.

When fishing dry flies in a lake or pond, you try to cast the fly to a fish that has risen to a real bug and let it sit there on the surface waiting for the fish to swim up and eat your fly. Some insects do skitter on the surface like caddis flies, so you can cast your fly and strip line to make your fly skitter like the real bug.

Once fish have been rising for bugs on the surface for some time, they will sometimes look up for food even when there is not a hatch going on. Fish will eat bugs like grasshoppers, crickets, beetles, and ants from the surface of the water during the summer months. This is a good time to fish with attractor dry flies.

But what are attractor dry flies, you might ask? They are flies that do not look like any real bug and sometimes have bright colors or sparkly stuff on them to attract fish.

Nymph Fishing

Any insect that lives in the water is called a nymph. Nymphs include bugs like stoneflies, caddis flies, mayflies, dragonflies, damselflies, and midges. In a river or stream the real nymphs live down in the rocks, mud, and plants. Sometimes bugs get washed off the rocks and plants by the water current. When this happens, they drift along in the water where the fish can eat them. Also, when it is time for them to hatch, the nymphs swim to the surface and the adult flying insect hatches out of its nymph body.

The nymph imitations you tie usually need to be fished down close to the bottom. To do this you need to use flies with weight in them in the form of a metal bead or weight tied into the fly. You can also add small sinkers called "spit shot" to your leader to aid in getting them down near the bottom. Since you cannot see the fish eating your fly when it is down so deep in the water, you should also use a strike indicator, or bobber, so that you can tell when the fish has eaten the fly.

To use a strike indicator, place it about two times the depth of the water above your fly (if the water you are fishing in is three feet deep, the strike indicator is placed on the leader six feet above the fly). The split shot is placed on the leader about eighteen to twenty-four inches above your fly. You'll need to cast your nymph fishing set-up upstream into the current where you think there might be fish. It is best to make fairly short casts so you have good control of your line and the drift of your fly. The split shot will pull the fly down into the water as it is drifting along in the current. It is very important to make sure the strike indicator is not dragging on the surface because that means your nymph is also dragging and does not look like the real bugs drifting in the current. If the strike indicator is dragging it will look like a small motor boat leaving a wake behind it.

When the strike indicator moves slightly, bounces up or down, or is pulled down under the water, it usually means a fish has eaten your fly.

Unfortunately, this can also mean you've caught a snag such as rocks, weeds, or—my least favorite—logs. You really have to pay attention to your strike indicator to make sure you do not miss any strikes. If the strike indicator moves even the smallest amount, set the hook. To set the hook, lift the tip of your rod with a quick movement. While you want to have a fast reaction and forceful hook set, be careful not to set the hook too hard or you might break the leader and lose the fish. You will get better at setting the hook the more you practice.

When the strike indicator gets downstream at the end of your line, it will start to drag. That means it is time to cast back upstream to start a new drag-free drift with the fly. Sometimes, you might get a strike right at the end of your drift because your fly will start to rise to the surface as it is dragging, which looks like a bug swimming up to the surface to hatch.

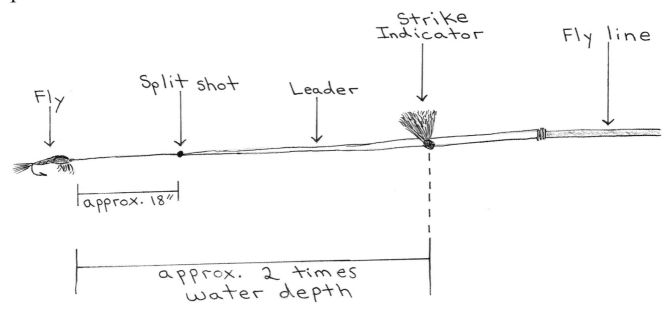

At times, you may be able to see the fish you are casting to in a river if the water is very clear. This is called "sight nymphing." When you sight fish, you need to pick a fish and cast your nymph right above the fish to allow it to sink to the depth the fish is at. Then the fun part is watching the fish to see if he eats that fly. There are times when you can see your fly and see the fish open its mouth to eat it. That is awesome when it happens and is honestly almost as exhilarating as watching a fish rise to a dry fly.

In lakes and ponds you can use split shot to help pull the fly down deep into the water. Usually you'll fish nymphs in lakes in ponds around structure because it is where the real bugs are living. Remember that in lakes and ponds, the nymphs are not drifting but crawling and swimming. When you make your presentation, let the fly sink then strip the fly line back into you with your non-casting hand to make it look like your nymph is swimming.

Streamer Fishing

Streamers are a type of fly that are supposed to look like small fish, worms, leeches, crawdads, and so on, which trout, bass, pike, musky, crappie, and other fish like to eat. When you fish streamers in rivers or lakes you usually cast them out and strip the fly line to make them look like they are swimming.

In rivers and streams, I prefer to use a floating fly line and a leader that is about six to seven feet long. Some streamer flies have a bead head or cone on the front of them to help them sink. Others have weight under the body to help them sink. Remember, split shot is always an option to add a little extra weight to get the fly down to the right depth. The most effective way to fish streamers that I have found is with an upstream, across stream, or downstream presentation.

First, make your cast, and then let the fly sink for a couple of seconds. Then start to strip the line. It is a good idea to vary the type of stripping patterns to find out what the fish like that particular day. You may have to strip the fly with short fast strips or maybe long slow strips and even mixing it up with fast and slow strips on each cast. It is important that you do not stop stripping the fly when you see a fish following it.

Imagine that you are a small minnow, just hanging out near the bank, eating small bugs floating by in the current. Then you decide you are going to check out a new place downstream behind the next rock. So you start cruising downstream when all of a sudden a large trout is coming up behind you very fast, with its mouth wide open. Do you just stop and let the big bad trout eat you? Or do you swim faster to try to get away? More than likely, you would swim faster trying to get away. Use this as an example of how to fish your streamer fly if you see a fish following it. It probably does not look natural when a trout or other predator fish is chasing a minnow and it just stops. You may even want to strip your streamer fly faster when you see a trout following it.

CHAPTER 6

FISH FOOD

As you learned earlier in this book, the flies you use are usually supposed to look like some type of food that fish eat. It could be bugs that live in the water or ones that live out of the water but manage to find their way into the fish's world. Other creatures like minnows, crayfish, snails, leeches, shrimp, frogs, and even mice are things that some fish will also eat.

Bugs That Live in the Water

There are many types of bugs that live in the water. Caddisflies, mayflies, midges, and stoneflies are some of the most common water insects you will see when you are out fly fishing. Other water bugs include dragonflies, damselflies, and beetles. When the bugs are actually living in the water, they are called nymphs. At some point the nymph will swim to the surface or crawl out of the water onto the bank, a rock, or a stick, and hatch into a flying insect. We use dry flies to imitate the flying adult bugs. Remember that nymphs sink and are fished underwater, and dry flies float and are fished on the surface of the water.

There are also many different types of aquatic insects found in lakes and ponds. Midges, mayflies, and caddis flies can be found in lakes and ponds but there are also dragonflies and damselflies. Aquatic beetles and aquatic worms are also in many lakes and ponds.

Some hatches can have millions of bugs, and while the fish will be very excited, they can be very picky about the type of bug they want to eat. As a result, it is best to attempt to match your flies with the hatching insects. If there are stoneflies hatching, for example, you will probably not have very good luck if you fished a fly that looked like a midge. A better choice would be to fish a stonefly nymph or stonefly dry fly if you see fish rising on the surface.

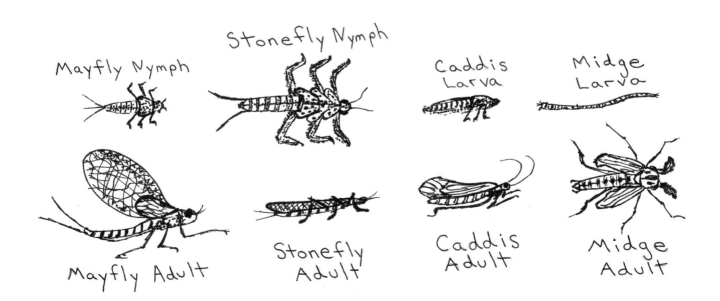

This is called "matching the hatch." Most aquatic bugs only live for a very short time as a flying insect out of the water. There are always nymphs in the water so most trout, bass, and panfish do the majority (almost 90 percent) of their feeding underwater on the nymphs and only a small amount of feeding on the surface unless there are hatches.

Bugs That Live out of the Water

The bugs that live on land but fall into the water, or are blown into the water by the wind, are called terrestrial insects. Terrestrial insects include grasshoppers, ants, beetles, crickets, ladybugs, and even moths. Trout, bass, and panfish really like to eat terrestrial insects. Usually terrestrials float so you should use dry flies to match them. Since these bugs are only around during the warmer months, they are not flies you need to have in your fly boxes during the winter season.

Terrestrial bugs can be blown by the wind out of the grass and bushes by a lake or stream and into the water. They can also be washed into the water from the rain. This often happens to ants on the edge of the water during a heavy rainstorm. When we walk around the edge of a lake or next to the bank of a river, we might even spook a grasshopper and they will jump right into the water and become food for the fish.

Beetle.

Grasshopper.

Other Fish Foods

Fish like to eat a lot of different things and will usually eat living things that are found in or around the water they live in. Most fish species are willing to prey on whatever is available to them including leeches, crayfish, snails, freshwater shrimp, frogs, and even mice!

Types of Artificial Flies

There are four primary types of flies used to fool and catch fish. It's important to learn about these different flies and when you would usually fish them. Each type of fly—dry flies, nymphs, wet flies, and streams—come in many different patterns. Patterns are specific flies based on their color or the list of materials used to make them. Fly patterns are like recipes you would use to cook a meal. An example would be a mayfly adult pattern. It could be a Blue Winged Olive or a Green Drake or a Pale Morning Dun. They all look like mayflies but each uses different materials and different colors to make them a very specific fly with a specific use.

Dry Flies

Dry flies are flies that float on the surface of the water and are generally used to match a specific flying insect that floats on the water. A perfect example of this is a grasshopper or stonefly adult. Another category of dry flies is the attractors, which do not look

Dry flies.

like any certain bug and usually have some bright colors or flashy material on them.

You should fish dry flies when you see fish rising and eating food that floats. However, attractor flies can be fished even when you do not see a hatch. Fish will look at the surface of the water if they get used to seeing bugs on the surface. You can use attractor flies to try and lure fish to the surface to eat your fly.

Nymphs

Nymphs are flies that sink and are used to match specific bugs that live in the water, like stoneflies, caddisflies, and damselflies, just to name a few. Like dry flies, there are also nymph patterns that are attractor flies. Some have metal beads on the front to help them sink or

Nymphs.

flashy material on them to make them more visible in discolored water. While they do not look exactly like once specific natural insect, they can often be useful at portraying multiple larva species that are present in the body of water that you are fishing. My former USA Youth Fly Fishing Team coach once used the analogy that if you were only given hamburgers to eat day after day and suddenly were offered an ice cream cone, chances are you would eat the ice cream cone because it is something different. Attractor flies do exactly that; they provide variation to what the fish sees in the river and can sometimes be the ticket to putting fish in the net.

Since the bugs that live in the water are always available for fish to eat, you can fish nymphs all year long in the rivers and streams, or in lakes, before any hatches start. In many cases, you do not see your nymphs down in the water because the split shot on your leader takes them down to the bottom where the real bugs live. If the water is extremely clear and you can see your flies and the fish you are casting to, you are using a fishing technique called sight nymphing.

Streamers

Streamers are flies that typically sink. We use them to match minnows or other small fish like baby trout or baby bluegill, leeches, crawdads, or just about anything that swims through the water. Streamers are very fun to fish because you can cast them out and strip the line back in to

Streamers.

make them swim like a small fish. Fish do not eat streamers; they attack them. For that reason, fishing with streamers can be some of the most exhilarating fly fishing, especially if you can see the fish following you streamer or if you are fishing from a boat. Streamer flies can be fished all year round because there are always small fish in the water that larger fish are interested in. Streamers are a good fly type to fish in places you have never been before since you can fish through different areas quickly with a streamer. This is because you are stripping the fly and fishing the water effectively with many casts in a short amount of time.

Wet Flies

Traditional wet flies are flies that sink, but many of them do not look like any type of bug. The majority of wet flies have bright colors and flashy material. They are pretty much attractor flies that sink. Wet flies are interesting in the sense that you fish them like a streamer with the downstream swinging method, or you can strip them most of the time. However, you will fish wet flies in

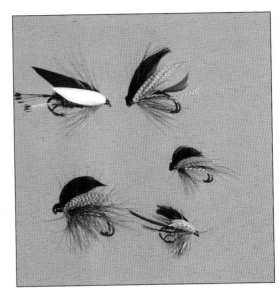

Wet flies.

smaller sizes similar to those of insects in a river, stream, or pond. The other technique that is commonly used when fishing the wet flies is to put split shot on the leader to help them sink, using a drag-free drift. When you let the wet fly swing across the river, you are imitating the action of a nymph that is trying to swim up through the fast current to the surface so it can hatch into the adult form. Strikes are often vicious with this method of fishing as fish have only a split second to react and eat the fly before it is too late and it disappears downstream.

CHAPTER 7

FLY FISHING IS MORE THAN CATCHING FISH

Fly fishing is an adventure that allows boys and girls like you to do many different things. I have been very lucky to have the opportunity to learn new things and to visit many new places because of fly fishing. I have been able to meet a lot of neat people who fly fish; people who tie flies; people who do fish artwork;

Northern pike drawn by me.

people who write books and articles about fly fishing; and the best part is that many have been willing to share their knowledge of the sport with me. Because of fly fishing I have been able to learn about fish and bugs, and I've learned about speaking in front of a group of people, photography, drawing and painting fish, and even about writing books.

One unique area of the sport to explore is fly tying. Fly tying is an art form just like fly fishing, but with fly tying, you are actually creating something that you will catch fish on. There are neat materials like feathers, fur, flash, beads, wire, tinsel, hooks, and thread that you are able to use to create a fly pattern. Fly tying does not require a lot of gear and tools so a few items such as a vise to hold the hook, a bobbin that holds the fly tying thread, scissors, and a half-hitch or whip finish tool to help tie the knot in the thread when you are finished tying the fly are all you really need to get started. Fly tying lets you invent new flies and be creative. Some people like this aspect of fly fishing so much that they will actually only tie flies and rarely do any fishing! The excitement in fly tying, for me, lies in the fact that I can dream up and create

Some fly-tying materials.

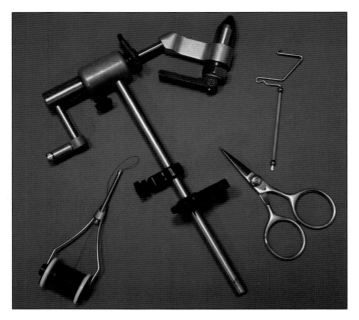

The basic tools for fly tying.

any sort of fly to fit my needs and, many times, go out and catch a fish on that fly.

I have always enjoyed learning about the different materials and, in some cases, the animals they come from. About nine years ago, I was offered a chance to see one of the largest chicken farms for fly tying feathers, Whiting Farms, and it was an offer I didn't want to turn down. At Whiting Farms, chicks are hatched and raised for the sole purpose of procuring fly-tying feathers. It was amazing to see the different stages of growth and also to see how the feathers developed from fuzz on the newly hatched chicks to gorgeous, shining, long feathers in almost every size and color a fly tier would need on the adult birds. After our tour, I had the honor of being asked to be Whiting Farm's youngest Pro Team member, and I even received a Whiting Farms shirt with my name on it to wear at fly-tying demonstrations.

Learning about bugs and different things that fish eat is also exciting. The study of bugs is called entomology and is basically a science class out in nature. You can go out and turn over rocks in a river or stream, or dig through the weeds in a lake with your hand, to discover the different types of bugs living in the water that you are fishing in. This can help make you become a better angler. There are also a lot of books that can teach you about different bugs and that can also help you figure out what kind of bugs you have found. You can put the insects you collect in glass jars with water to watch them. When I was younger, my dad helped me install an aquarium in our house with bugs and some small fish called sculpins (they live on the bottom of many streams and rivers and are a favorite food of predator fish).

Tying flies at a fly-fishing show when I was eight or nine years old.

Fly fishing allows you to meet cool people from all over the world who also like to fly fish. After having more than eleven years of traveling, shows, and fishing events under my belt, the list of incredible people I have met is endless. There are a handful of people I've met that I have been fortunate enough to make memories with, which I will carry for the rest of my life. In Japan, I have a friend named Masa Katsumata. When he invited my dad and me to visit him and spend a week fishing for different trout and char species in Japan, I found myself entering a whole new fishing world where microscopic flies and selective fish awaited. I learned a great deal

Jens teaching me how to tie flies in your hands.

on tactical fishing techniques from Masa as well as made a friend for life.

A fellow fly tier by the name of Jens Pilgaard taught me how to tie flies without a vise to hold the hook by using just your fingers—like people used to do when tying flies a long time ago. Jens even makes some of his own hooks that he uses to tie flies. I thought this old fashioned way of tying was so cool that I continue to try to learn it to this day!

Aside from fishing and fly tying, I have also picked up a few tips and tricks in areas such as art and photography through my interest in fly fishing. My friend Jeff Currier, who lives in Idaho, is an awesome fish artist. He taught me how to sketch fish while we were at a fly-fishing show at the University of Wyoming. Now

I spend a lot of time drawing fish with colored pencils, pens, and even watercolors. While every fish is a little, or sometimes large, treasure, there is always a fish that stands out from the rest, and thanks to digital cameras, I am able to take a picture of that fish and then I try to draw it on the car ride home based on the picture I took.

Over the years, I have collected hundreds of flies made by different fly tiers from all over the world—most of whom I meet at fly-fishing or fly-tying shows. There are too many fly tiers to mention all of those who have helped with my fly tying skills and have generously given me one of their flies. Some of these people I only get to see once a year, and it is fun to talk to them about the fishing they have been doing or the flies they have been tying in the year that's passed.

Our family friends Pat and Carol Oglesby, who live in Grand Junction, Colorado, are some of my favorite fishing buddies. We've spent a lot of time fishing together. They have taught me about the outdoors, wildlife, photography, and the history of the Gunnison River, which is among my favorite rivers to fish in Colorado. They also got me my first pair of high-tech waders when I was big enough to upgrade from knee-high rubber boots.

One of the coolest things about fly fishing is that I get to travel to new places and see some really cool things when I go fishing. When I still lived in Colorado, road trips gave me the opportunity to watch out the window for wildlife like deer, elk, eagles, and even bears. A couple of times, my dad took me to Rocky Mountain National Park to fish for greenback cutthroat trout. It was a long ride from our house, but it was worth it to catch these awesome trout. Sometimes I take airplanes to go fishing or to attend a sportsman's show where I will be tying flies or giving presentations about fly fishing. One of my very first trips on an airplane was to Alaska and is a trip I will never forget. I got to see moose, bears, and eagles while I was there. Oh yeah—I did catch a few fish, too!

I think the best thing about fly fishing is the time I get to spend with my family enjoying the outdoors. I can help my younger sisters with casting and landing fish, landing fish for my mom, taking pictures for them, making lunches, playing with the dogs, or even starting a friendly competition against my dad to see who can catch the most fish or present a fly in the most difficult of areas. All of these aspects of my fishing trips add to the adventure and even if we fish just a little bit or do not even catch a single fish, it is still a great time. Every fly fisher has his or her own idea of why they want to fly fish. For me, it is much more than just catching fish—it is all about adventure.

CHAPTER 8

THE ADVENTURE CONTINUES— MAKING FLY FISHING WHAT YOU WANT

One of the reasons that I wanted to start writing books and attending fly-fishing shows was to try to get more kids interested in the sport of fly fishing. I never enjoyed being the only youth angler at these events, and it has been thrilling to see an increasing number of kids attending fly-fishing events—and to see those who are out fishing who have grown over the past few years. In this chapter, I hope to show some more of the different facets of fly fishing because probably the most unique aspect of this sport is that it has something for everyone.

Especially in the past decade, fly fishing has become more than just a peaceful pastime that kids have heard about from dads and grandfathers as they recount times of fishing for trout on tranquil streams. Instead, urban fly fishing for carp, warm water fishing for bass, pike, musky, and sunfish, as well as saltwater fishing (which has grown in popularity thanks to legendary pioneers such as Lefty Kreh, Stu Apte, and Flip Pallot, who helped many people realize that even the oceans are a place for fly fishermen) have opened up a whole new world of fly fishing that is just waiting to be explored. Besides the diversity of fish species or locations to fish, which adds lots of excitement to the sport, there are also new activities emerging that add a completely different edge to the fly-fishing scene.

Vladi and me with my first trout on the Polish nymphing tactics.

I am sure that many of you kids and teenagers, such as myself, who are reading this book enjoy mainstream sports of some kind or, at the very least, competition. Fifty years ago, the idea of any sort of organized competition taking place in fly fishing would have been crazy, but with the birth of competitive fly-fishing leagues, organizations, and teams across the globe, this has now become a cutting-edge part of this wonderful sport. I was first introduced to competitive fly-fishing techniques by a gentleman named Vladi

Trezbuni, who lives in Poland, while at a local fly-fishing show near my old home in Montrose, Colorado. I was about ten years old when I met Vladi and after a day of learning about Polish and Czech nymphing methods, I decided that this was an area of fly fishing I wanted to explore more.

I fished in my first competition with four other youth anglers in Colorado in 2011. At this tournament—The America Cup International Fly Fishing Competition—we were the only youth team to attend. While we didn't win any trophies or medals, competing allowed me to learn a lot from other anglers from around the world, as well as to find out about the USA Youth Fly Fishing Team that I later became a member of and held a position on until 2014.

My first experience with team USA, and still probably one of my favorite competitions, was at the youth nationals in State College, Pennsylvania, in 2012. There, I competed with twenty-three other youth anglers and spent a few days pre-fishing with friends and other anglers who had been part of the competitive scene for a couple years already. In this time, I was able to refine my skills even more as well as experience how intense fly-fishing competitions can be. Over the course of two and a half days, we fished four, three-hour-long sessions in which each angler was given a section of the river to fish. The goal was to catch as many fish as possible over twenty centimeters long during the time period. While it might not seem

Fishing a run during the 2013 Youth Fly Fishing Nationals in North Carolina.

like it would be too exciting by just the explanation, it becomes very intense once you begin fishing.

Now, obviously, competition is not everyone's cup of tea, and recently I have even found myself becoming more intrigued by others areas of the sport. I have always enjoyed traveling, and so my first international trip was absolutely incredible, not to mention that it was based around fishing. Back in 2006, my dad and I were invited to spend a week in Japan with a friend of ours and to do some fishing on local spring creeks as well as in Tokyo bay for Japanese sea bass (as I mentioned in the previous chapter). While this was certainly an amazing trip, I never dreamed that I'd get to go back to Japan, but I was proven wrong when, three years later, I was invited by the board of tourism in Japan to teach elementary school students how to fly fish as well as to

Fly fishing in Japan is cool, and the fish there are absolutely gorgeous, which makes it even more fun.

attend a small fly-fishing show on the northernmost island of Japan named Hokkaido.

On this trip, I spent two weeks in Japan and in that time, I not only was able to fish a lot of the local rivers from my first trip, but I also added a new venue to my list: Lake Akan. Lake Akan was especially unique and special to fish because it is one of the largest volcanic lakes in the world. Lake Akan is also home to a special species of white-spotted char that can only be found in this lake (believe it or not)!

The final few days were spent back in Tokyo Bay fishing for Japanese sea bass. Our guide took us to a handful of different spots including the manmade islands at the mouth of Tokyo Bay, which were used during World War II as a lookout spot for enemy ships and submarines that might attempt to enter the area. The islands

My largest Japanese sea bass!

have since been repurposed by the fish as a perfect hiding place, and there were plenty of them willing to hit our flies.

On our final day of fishing, we stayed in close to the shipping docks and fished alongside the Herculean shipping boats and the loading docks which is where I landed my personal best sea bass, weighing nearly fifteen pounds and measuring a little over forty inches long. This sea bass was the second largest the captain had managed to get into his boat and was a perfect way to end the trip.

Finding the perfect niche in fly fishing for you doesn't necessarily require traveling halfway around the world or investing a bunch of time into practicing and preparing for competition. Some of the best experiences I've had fly fishing were only a few minutes away from my house on local ponds and streams—fishing with friends or even a quick solo trip in between swim practices. Most recently,

I moved to Midland, Michigan, where my family is surrounded by a handful of small rivers that are home to smallmouth bass, carp, pike, musky, white bass, and many other fish. It has been a blessing to have great fisheries right in my backyard. Within the first year of living here, I had made fly-fishing memories that will last a life time. I've also recently entered into a new stage of my fly-fishing journey: finding and exploring new fishing areas.

When starting your fly-fishing adventures, after learning the basics you've been taught in this book, play around with different aspects of the sport and find the part of it that really interests you. Over time, your interests might change and there will be different areas of fly fishing that become more appealing to you. And that's okay. It is this aspect, in fact, that keeps me fly fishing more than anything else— that I'm always learning and that, regardless of what I've seen or done, there is always another fly-fishing adventure awaiting me.

Fly fishing near home has provided me with some great opportunities, such as catching king salmon from the Great Lakes.

INDEX